-ub as in tub

Nancy Tuminelly

Consulting Editor Monica Marx, M.A./Reading Specialist

ABDO
Publishing Company

Published by SandCastle™, an imprint of ABDO Publishing Company, 4940 Viking Drive, Edina, Minnesota 55435.

Printed in the United States.

Credits
Edited by: Pam Price
Curriculum Coordinator: Nancy Tuminelly
Cover and Interior Design and Production: Mighty Media
Photo Credits: Brand X Pictures, Comstock, Corbis Images, Digital Vision, Hemera, Donna Day/ImageState, PhotoDisc, Stockbyte

Library of Congress Cataloging-in-Publication Data

Tuminelly, Nancy, 1952-
    -Ub as in tub / Nancy Tuminelly.
        p. cm. -- (Word families. Set IV)
    Summary: Introduces, in brief text and illustrations, the use of the letter combination "ub" in such words as "tub," "snub," "cub," and "grub."
    ISBN 1-59197-242-6
    1. Readers (Primary) [1. Vocabulary. 2. Reading.] I. Title.

PE1119 .T834 2003
428.1--dc21
                                                        2002038640

SandCastle™ books are created by a professional team of educators, reading specialists, and content developers around five essential components that include phonemic awareness, phonics, vocabulary, text comprehension, and fluency. All books are written, reviewed, and leveled for guided reading, early intervention reading, and Accelerated Reader® programs and designed for use in shared, guided, and independent reading and writing activities to support a balanced approach to literacy instruction.

Let Us Know

After reading the book, SandCastle would like you to tell us your stories about reading. What is your favorite page? Was there something hard that you needed help with? Share the ups and downs of learning to read. We want to hear from you! To get posted on the ABDO Publishing Company Web site, send us e-mail at:

sandcastle@abdopub.com

SandCastle Level: Transitional

-ub Words

club

cub

hub

shrub

sub

tub

3

Liz is in the swim club.

A baby lion is called
a cub.

The center of the wheel
is called a hub.

Mom is trimming the
shrub.

A sub sandwich is good
for lunch.

Patty and Jill play in
the tub.

Bub the Cub

There once was a cub
whose name was Bub.

One day while Ann
was eating a sub,

thud!

she heard a noise
come from the tub.

In the tub
she found a cub.

Ann said, "I think
I'll call you Bub."

Ann took Bub
out of the tub.

Then she gave Bub
a little rub.

Ann went back to
eat her sub.

She gave a taste
to Bub the cub.

Bub licked his lips
when he finished the grub.

Bub went out
and sat by a shrub.

He was such
a cute little cub,
that Ann brought Bub
to meet her club!

The -ub Word Family

club	scrub
cub	shrub
dub	snub
flub	stub
grub	sub
hub	tub
rub	

Glossary

Some of the words in this list may have more than one meaning. The meaning listed here reflects the way the word is used in the book.

cub   a baby lion

grub   a slang term for food

hub   the center of a circular object; the center of a wheel

shrub   a short plant with woody stems

About SandCastle™

A professional team of educators, reading specialists, and content developers created the SandCastle™ series to support young readers as they develop reading skills and strategies and increase their general knowledge. The SandCastle™ series has four levels that correspond to early literacy development in young children. The levels are provided to help teachers and parents select the appropriate books for young readers.

Emerging Readers
(no flags)

Beginning Readers
(1 flag)

Transitional Readers
(2 flags)

Fluent Readers
(3 flags)

These levels are meant only as a guide. All levels are subject to change.

To see a complete list of SandCastle™ books and other nonfiction titles from ABDO Publishing Company, visit www.abdopub.com or contact us at:

4940 Viking Drive, Edina, Minnesota 55435 • 1-800-800-1312 • fax: 1-952-831-1632